Answer Book

PUPIL BOOK

PB ■ 1

1 a 17 437
b 22 024
c 40 300
d 70 087
e 100 216
f 560 030
g 1 621 217

2 a thirty-five thousand two hundred and sixty-four
b forty-six thousand and seventeen
c fifty thousand and eighty-one
d two hundred and seventy-three thousand and twenty-one
e four hundred and sixty thousand and two
f one million five hundred and eighty thousand three hundred

3 a add 6000
b subtract 200
c add 3000
d subtract 50 000

4 a smallest: 1 234 589 largest: 9 854 321
b one million two hundred and thirty four thousand five hundred and eighty-nine; nine million eight hundred and fifty-four thousand three hundred and twenty-one

? **a** Largest: 9531, smallest: 248
b nine thousand five hundred and thirty-one; two hundred and forty-eight

PB ■ 2

1 a 6520
b 42 170
c 70 860

2 a 80 600
b 537 200
c 880 000

3 a 3560
b 56 900
c 34 720
d 519 800

4 a 760
b 900
c 301

5 a 43
b 60
c 80

6 a 40 000, 4 000 000, 400 000, 4 000 000, 400 000, 40 000 000, 4 000 000, 40 000 (starting number)
b Whatever the starting number or starting box you get back to the starting number.

? 40 000, 400, 40, 4000, 400, 4000, 400, 40 000 (starting number)

PB ■ 3

1 a <
b >
c <
d >

2 a Zog
b Zap
c Zag
d Zep

3 Possible numbers include: 85 421, 85 412, 85 241, …

4 The answers should be multiples of 100 between 24 100 (halved = 12 050, i.e. more than 12 000) and 24 900 (doubled = 49 800, i.e. less than 50 000)

(?) The answers should be multiples of 100 between 8 600 (doubled = 17 200, i.e. more than 17 000) and 13 900 (halved = 6950, i.e. less than 7000)

PB ■ 4

1 *a* Nile
   b Mississippi
   c Amazon

2 *a* Tutunendo
   b Debundseha
   c Debundseha

3 *a* Jo
   b Ali
   c Dev
   d 5500
   e Rob

PB ■ 5

1 Reasonable estimations of the following:
   a shuttles at 500 and 750 km
   b shuttles at 500 and 1500 km
   c shuttles at 2000 and 4000 km
   d shuttles at 3000 and 9000 km

2 Child's estimates:
   a 49 1p coins
   b 80 beats a minute; 5000 beats an hour; 120 000 beats a day

PB ■ 6

1 Reasonable estimations of the following:

   a 150 km
   b 300 km
   c 100 km
   d 300 km
   e 100 km
   f 500 km
   g 2000 km
   h 4500 km
   i 2500 km
   j 7500 km

2 *a* $\frac{4}{5}$ full
   b $\frac{3}{4}$ full
   c $\frac{1}{3}$ full
   d $\frac{3}{10}$ full
   e $\frac{9}{10}$ full
   f $\frac{5}{8}$ full

(?) The players would have less of a chance of exactly estimating what the number is.

PB ■ 7

1 *a* 2480
   b 6240
   c 8660
   d 9100
   e 7100
   f 8000

2 *a* 3700
   b 4300
   c 4600
   d 6700
   e 8000
   f 10 000

PB ■ 8

1 *a* $1, 0, -1$
   b $0, -2, -4$
   c $-5, -10, -15$
   d $-6, -9, -12$
   e $-1, 1, 3$
   f $-14, -17, -20$

2
- **a** −3, 1, 4
- **b** −6, −3, 3
- **c** −20, −10, 0, 8
- **d** −19, −18, −17, 16
- **e** −12, −7, −4, 0
- **f** −11, −9, −7, −6

3 Possible answers include:
−8, −7, −4, −3, −1, 0, 2
−8, −7, −4, −2, −1, 0, 2
−8, −7, −4, −3, −1, 1, 2
−8, −7, −4, −2, −1, 1, 2
−8, −6, −4, −2, −1, 1, 2
−8, −6, −4, −2, −1, 0, 2
−8, −5, −4, −2, −1, 1, 2
−8, −5, −4, −2, −1, 0, 2

PB ■ 9

1
- **a** −8°
- **b** 0°

2
- **a** 10°
- **b** −5°
- **c** −2°
- **d** 2°

3
- **a** 39°
- **b** 24°
- **c** 30°
- **d** 22°

PB ■ 9

1
- **a** 25 50 75 **100 125 150 175 200 225 250 275** 300
- **b** 1000 975 950 **925 900 875 850 825 800 775 750** 725
- **c** 20 45 70 95 **120 145 170 195 220 245 270 295** 320
- **d** 200 **175 150 125 100 75 50 25 0** −25 −50 −75
- **e** −25 **0 25 50** 75 100 125 **150 175 200 225**
- **f** 250 225 200 175 **150 125 100 75 50 25 0**

2

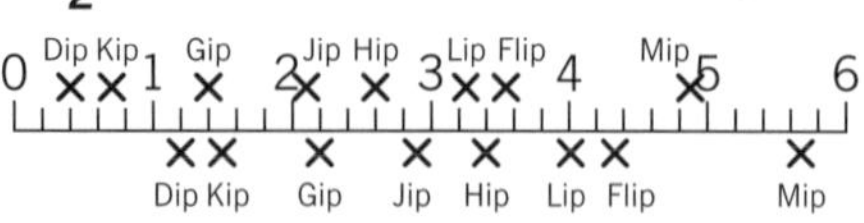

PB ■ 11

1 Any five pairs of numbers where one is odd and one is even.

2 The numbers either side of the counters are always even. The covered number is always odd.

PB ■ 12

1 846, 1358, 262, 1 000 000, 2004

2
- **a** 100 and its multiples can always be divided by 4.
- **b** 264, 416, 172

PB ■ 13

1 Any 3 for a to e:
- **a** 2×24, 3×16, 4×12, 6×8, 1×48
- **b** 1×12, 2×6, 3×4
- **c** 2×10, 4×5, 1×20
- **d** 6×6, 2×18, 3×12, 1×36
- **e** 1×32, 2×16, 4×8

PB ■ 14

1
- **a** $\frac{3}{5}$
- **b** 2
- **c** 8
- **d** $\frac{6}{5}$
- **e** 5
- **f** 4
- **g** The numerator is smaller than the denominator in the first 3 fractions, and larger than the denominator in the last 3.

2 a $4\frac{1}{2}$

  b $\frac{14}{5} = 2\frac{4}{5}$

  c $1\frac{2}{10}$

  d $1\frac{2}{3}$

  e $2\frac{3}{4}$

  f $1\frac{5}{8} = \frac{13}{8}$

3 a There are no other pairs of improper fractions with a sum of 3.

  b
$\frac{4}{3} + \frac{8}{3} = 4$ $\frac{4}{3} + \frac{11}{3} = 5$

$\frac{4}{3} + \frac{14}{3} = 6$ $\frac{4}{3} + \frac{17}{3} = 7$

$\frac{5}{3} + \frac{7}{3} = 4$ $\frac{5}{3} + \frac{10}{3} = 5$

$\frac{5}{3} + \frac{13}{3} = 6$ $\frac{5}{3} + \frac{16}{3} = 7$

$\frac{7}{3} + \frac{8}{3} = 5$ $\frac{7}{3} + \frac{11}{3} = 6$

$\frac{7}{3} + \frac{14}{3} = 7$ $\frac{8}{3} + \frac{10}{3} = 6$

$\frac{8}{3} + \frac{13}{3} = 7$ $\frac{10}{3} + \frac{11}{3} = 7$

Fractions can also be written in reverse order.

The larger the denominator the greater the number of pairs of improper fractions that can be made for a whole number sum.

PB ■ 15

1 a 1

  b $\frac{6}{10}$

  c $\frac{2}{5}$ l $\frac{3}{5}$

2 a $<$

  b $<$

  c $>$

  d $>$

  e $<$

  f $=$

  g $=$

  h $>$

  i $<$

3 a $\frac{4}{8}, \frac{5}{10}, \frac{6}{12}, \frac{7}{14}$

  b $\frac{4}{12}, \frac{5}{15}, \frac{6}{18}, \frac{7}{21}$

  c $\frac{4}{16}, \frac{5}{20}, \frac{6}{24}, \frac{7}{28}$

  d $\frac{4}{20}, \frac{5}{25}, \frac{6}{30}, \frac{7}{35}$

  e $\frac{4}{40}, \frac{5}{50}, \frac{6}{60}, \frac{7}{70}$

f Statements such as: the numerators go up in ones; the numerators are consecutive; in the halves family; the denominators go up in 2s; in the quarters family, the denominators go up in 4s; all the fractions in the halves family are equivalent to $\frac{1}{2}$.

4 Child's own work.

PB ■ 16

1 a 3

  b 12

  c 5

  d 1

  By dividing by the denominator.

2 a 9

  b 24

  c 20

  d 7

  By dividing by the denominator then multiplying the answer (quotient) by the numerator.

3 a $16 \div 4 = 4$

  b $\frac{21}{7} = 3$

  c $18 \div 6 = 3$

  d $\frac{13}{2} = 6\frac{1}{2}$

4 a $\frac{3}{7}$

  b $\frac{2}{6}$ or $\frac{1}{3}$

  c 2

  d $1\frac{3}{4}$

5 Child's own word problems for

  a $\frac{12}{3} = 4$

  b $\frac{15}{4} = 3\frac{3}{4}$

PB ■ 17

1 a 20 ml

  b $\frac{2}{3}$

2 a 50 ml

  b 20 ml

  c $\frac{1}{5}$

3 45 ml of kiwi juice, 30 ml of strawberry juice and 15 ml of orange juice

4 a and c Juice combinations
b and c Proportion of each juice

Lime, cherry and lemon	$\frac{1}{5} + \frac{3}{10} + \frac{1}{2}$
Kiwi, cherry and lemon	$\frac{1}{5} + \frac{3}{10} + \frac{1}{2}$
Kiwi, strawberry and lemon	$\frac{1}{5} + \frac{3}{10} + \frac{1}{2}$
Lime, strawberry and lemon	$\frac{1}{5} + \frac{3}{10} + \frac{1}{2}$
Orange, coconut and kiwi	$\frac{2}{5} + \frac{2}{5} + \frac{1}{5}$
Orange, coconut and lime	$\frac{2}{5} + \frac{2}{5} + \frac{1}{5}$
Orange, strawberry, cherry	$\frac{2}{5} + \frac{3}{10} + \frac{3}{10}$
Coconut, cherry, strawberry	$\frac{2}{5} + \frac{3}{10} + \frac{3}{10}$

? Cherry, strawberry, lime and kiwi:
$\frac{3}{10} + \frac{3}{10} + \frac{1}{5} + \frac{1}{5}$

PB ■ 18

1 a 1 tenth or 10 hundredths
b 1 unit or 10 tenths (or 100 hundredths)
c 6 tenths or 60 hundredths
d 3 tenths and 5 hundredths or 35 hundredths
e 2 tenths and 8 hundredths or 28 hundredths

2 a $+ 0.04$ recorded as either £0·04 or 4p
b $\times 10$
c $+ 0.54$ recorded as either £0·54 or 54p
d $\div 100$

3 a 2·95 m
b 340 cm or 3·4 m
c 6·25 m or 625 cm

4 1·8 m, 2·0 m, 2·2 m, 2·4 m, 2·6 m, 2·8 m, 3 m

PB ■ 19

1 a 4
b 8
c 13
d 16
e 13

2 a 2 m
b 17 m
c 8 m
d 4 m
e 8 m

3 a £1
b £2
c £2
d £26
e £18

4 a 0·02
b 0·41
c 0·17
d 0·09
e 0·75

5 Check the patterns with the child and ask them to explain what they have discovered. Check that any written statements make sense. Children should be encouraged to record their work logically, recording one fraction family per column and making clear separations between the families so that the results can be clearly seen.

PB ■ 20

1 a 20%
b $\frac{30}{100}$
c $\frac{50}{100}$
d $\frac{25}{100}$
e $\frac{75}{100}$
f $\frac{5}{100}$

2 a $\frac{2}{10} = 20\%$
b $\frac{50}{100} = \frac{5}{10}$

c $\frac{4}{10} = 40\%$

d 70%

e $\frac{30}{100} = 30\%$

f $\frac{6}{10} = 60\%$

3 a blue 50%, pink 40%, silver 10%

   b yellow 25%, red 75%;
     green 30%, purple 5%,
     orange 15%, pink 40%, silver 10%

? 3 ways:
yellow 25%, green 30%, puple 5%,
pink 40%;
blue 50%, green 30%, purple 5%,
orange 15%.
yellow 25%, blue 50%, orange
15%, silver 10%.

PB ■ 21

1 a 10%

   b 0·25

   c 20%

   d $\frac{4}{10}$ (or $\frac{2}{5}$) = 40%

   e 0·75 = 75%

   f $\frac{9}{10} = 0\cdot9$

2 A Texas Instruments TI−106
calculator gives these results:
$1 \div 100\ \%$ gives 1 in the display
$2 \div 100\ \%$ gives 2 in the display,
etc...
The calculator goes straight to the
percentage result without giving the
hundredths first and is actually
calculating: $1 \div 100 \times 100 = 1$
For $1 \div 10\ \%$ it gives 10 in the
display for the same reason. Pressing
'=' instead of '%' gives the expected
decimal fractions. Challenge children
to get from 0·01 in the display to 1
and from 0·1 to 10 in one operation.
They should then be able to explain
what the % button is doing.

? 10, 20, 30 ...

PB ■ 22

1 a $\frac{10}{100}$

   b 50%

   c $\frac{1}{4}$

   d 40%

   e 75%

   f $\frac{1}{5}$

2 a 2·5 kg

   b 4 kg

   c £1·50

   d 6 m

   e £12

   f 4 m

3 a 0·8 m, 6 m, 0·4 m

   b 0·8 m

4 a 8 kg

   b 20 kg

   c 12 kg

   d There is no sand left

PB ■ 23

1 a 5634

   b 5814

   c 5664

   d 6134

   e 5134

   f 4834

   g 6234

   h 4934

2 Multiple answers are possible.

3 a 83

   b 1064

   c 65

   d 110

? 79/18/46 = 143,
7/91/84/6 = 188,
791/846 = 1637,
7/9/1/84/6 = 107,
79/1/8/46 = 134

PB ■ 24

1 a 643

   b 708

c 588
d 806
e 660
f 984
g 888
h 579

2 Possible answers include:
217 + 142 = 359,
217 + 359 = 576,
142 + 359 = 501,
359 − 142 = 217,
359 − 217 = 142,
217 − 142 = 75

3 88 + 261 = 349
215 + 261 = 476
88 + 476 = 564
215 + 349 = 564
and corresponding subtractions

4 smallest difference:
512 − 496 = 16
greatest difference:
965 − 124 = 841

PB ■ 25

1 *a* 0·9 l
b 0·3 l
c 0·4 l
d 0·5 l
e 0·8 l

2 Possible answers include:
1·3 + 8·7 = 10
1·4 + 8·6 = 10
1·6 + 8·4 = 10
…
4·8 + 5·2 = 10
4·9 + 5·1 = 10

(?) The pairs of numbers after the decimal point would remain the same but the whole part of the numbers would decrease.

PB ■ 26

1 *a* 100
b 100
c 100
d 56
e 35
f 62

2 Possible answers include:

350	150	500
100	650	250
550	200	250

PB ■ 27

1 Count up to current year from question.

2 1012, 8, 1995, 1982, 2985, 1995

3 *a* 2020
b 3011
c Yonk and Xtra 6017
d Urgo and Zap 12

PB ■ 28

1 *a* 178
b 299
c 412
d 310
e 301
f 683
g 492
h 458

2 *a* 432, 348, 380
b 562, 651, 578

3 442 = 525 − 83
507 = 459 + 48
555 = 638 − 83
432 = 459 − 27
592 = 525 + 67

PB ■ 29

1 a 3·2
  b 4·8
  c 7·4
  d 5·4
  e 6·7
  f 1·8

2 a 7·1, 7·3; 10·5, 10·7, 10·9;
    12·7, 12·9, 13·1
  b They are a sequence.

3 a 1·7 + 1·8
  b 1·5 + 1·6
  c 2·5 + 2·6
  d 1·8 + 1·9
  e 3·1 + 3·2
  f 3·3 + 3·4
  g 3·5 + 3·6

4 Multiplying the middle number by 3
  will give the answer.

(?) The sum of 5 consecutive numbers
    can be found by multiplying the
    middle number by 5. It is more
    complicated to establish a similar
    rule for an even number of numbers,
    as there is no 'middle' number.

PB ■ 30

1 a 499
  b 653
  c 718
  d 377
  e 511
  f 556

2 +82, +41, −102, −195, +99,
  +19, −101, +79, −21

PB ■ 31

1 a 26
  b 22
  c 28
  d 30

2 a Shark = 21, Zebra = 25,
    Tiger = 32, Whale = 22

b Possible answers include:
    5 = bat, 6 = cat,
    14 = cow,
    17 = dog

3 a 90
  b 210

(?) a 140
    b 260

PB ■ 32

1 a 624
  b 979
  c 1227
  d 1488
  e 1334
  f 1095
  g 1531
  h 1160

2 230 + 280 = 510,
  430 + 110 = 540,
  890 − 370 = 520,
  890 − 360 = 530,
  910 − 370 = 540,
  910 − 360 = 550,
  980 − 470 = 510,
  980 − 460 = 520,
  980 − 430 = 550

3 a 500 + 400 + 600
    500 + 100 + 300 + 600
    200 + 400 + 300 + 600
    200 + 100 + 400 + 300 + 500
    500 + 100 + 400 + 500
    500 + 100 + 100 + 300 + 500
  b Child's own work.

PB ■ 33

1 a 0·2 kg
  b 0·7 kg
  c 0·8 kg
  d 0·9 kg
  e 0·6 kg
  f 0·4 kg

2 a 63
  b 509
  c 512
  d 400
  e 72
  f 123

3 Mon 189, Tues 220, Wed 228, Thurs 173, Fri 77.

PB ■ 34

1 a 1062
  b 1222
  c 9429
  d 7246

2 a 1201
  b 1272
  c 3710
  d 6043

3 Underlined digits indicate changes from question grid.

4 5 8 <u>4</u>
6 <u>9</u> 8 0
1 4 <u>4</u> 0
5 <u>2</u> 7 <u>3</u>

PB ■ 35

1 a
```
   254
 + 688
 -----
   942
```

b
```
   753
 + 137
 -----
   890
```

c
```
   649
 + 255
 -----
   904
```

d
```
   547
 + 369
 -----
   916
```

e
```
   984
 + 274
 -----
  1258
```

f
```
   621
 + 548
 -----
  1169
```

g
```
   429
 + 433
 -----
   862
```

2 a There are 8 possible ways, including the example.

```
   012
 + 210
 -----
   222
```
```
   234
 + 432
 -----
   666
```
```
   345
 + 543
 -----
   888
```
```
   456
 + 654
 -----
  1110
```
```
   567
 + 765
 -----
  1332
```
```
   678
 + 876
 -----
  1554
```
```
   789
 + 987
 -----
  1776
```

b The answers are all multiples of 222.

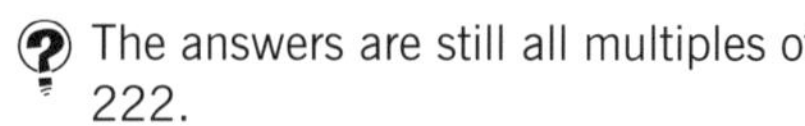 The answers are still all multiples of 222.

PB ■ 36

1 6 + 542 + 2347 = 2895
814 + 28 + 9 = 851
59 + 1791 + 348 = 2198
6 + 814 + 59 = 879
542 + 28 + 1791 = 2361
2347 + 9 + 348 = 2704
Grid total = 5944

2 a £1783
b £1819
c £707
d a chair, a desk and a printer

3 564 + 787 + 385 = 1736
564 + 787 + 439 = 1790
787 + 385 + 439 = 1611
564 + 385 + 439 = 1388
Numbers can also be written in
other orders.

❓ 564 + 787 = 1351
564 + 385 = 949
564 + 439 = 1003
787 + 385 = 1172
787 + 439 = 1226
385 + 439 = 824
Numbers can also be written in
reverse order.

PB ■ 37

1 a £23·98
b £17·44
c £13·59
d £20·85
e £17·40
f £33·46

2 a Possible answers include:
2·4 + 6·7 = 9·1,
2·6 + 7·8 = 10·4,
2·7 + 8·4 = 11·1, …
b Reversing the units or tenths in a
pair gives different numbers but
the same answer, for example:
2·6 + 4·7 = 7·3
2·7 + 4·6 = 7·3

3 0·44 kg + 1·1 kg + 0·28 kg = 1·82 kg
0·44 kg + 1·1 kg + 4·55 kg = 6·09 kg
0·44 kg + 1·1 kg + 3·8 kg = 5·34 kg
0·44 kg + 0·28 kg + 4·55 kg = 5·27 kg
0·44 kg + 0·28 kg + 3·8 kg = 4·52 kg
0·44 kg + 4·55 kg + 3·8 kg = 8·79 kg
1·1 kg + 0·28 kg + 4·55 kg = 5·93 kg
1·1 kg + 0·28 kg + 3·8 kg = 5·18 kg
1·1 kg + 4·55 kg + 3·8 kg = 9·45 kg
0·28 kg + 4·55 kg + 3·8 kg = 8·63 kg

❓ 0·44 kg + 1·1 kg + 0·28 kg
+ 4·55 kg = 6·37 kg
0·44 kg + 1·1 kg + 0·28 kg
+ 3·8 kg = 5·62 kg
1·1 kg + 0·28 kg + 4·55 kg
+ 3·8 kg = 9·73 kg
0·44 kg + 0·28 kg + 4·55 kg
+ 3·8 kg = 9·07 kg
0·44 kg + 1·1 kg + 4·55 kg
+ 3·8 kg = 9·89 kg

PB ■ 38

1 a 467
b 73
c 536
d 383
e 269
f 222
g 427
h 407
i 452

PB ■ 39

1 a   739
− 258
481

b   925
− 363
562

c   483
− 249
234

   d   614
       −485
        129

   e   960
       −328
        632

   f   804
       −623
        181

   g   542
       −296
        246

2 Child's own work.
The differences are all multiples of 9.

? If the first and last digits are the
same, the difference is 0.

PB ■ 40

1 *a* 3·3
b 7·6
c 1·7
d 4·12
e 2·13
f 3·18

2 *a* £0·58 £0·91 £0·23 £0·37
£0·68 £1·56
b telescope
c Space Place by £0·35

3 0·75 sec, 1·87 sec. 0·55 sec,
0·41 sec

PB ■ 41

1 *a* £7·15
b £7·55
c £8·40
d £11·50
e £43·58
f £37·80

2 *a* 12
b 12·999999
c 13·999999
d 15
e 15·999999
f 16·999999
g Some of the output numbers are
not the same as the original
number, as would be expected,
but are 0·000001 less.
h This happens because the first
answer is not exact (the calculator
cannot show $\frac{1}{3}$ accurately) and
this error is carried through to the
final answer.

3 The output number should equal
half the input number plus 1 i.e. it
should be either a whole number or
a decimal number ending in ·5.
However, a calculator only produces
an exact answer to the calculation
when the input number is 2 less
than a multiple of 6. In other cases
rounding errors lead to answers that
end ·4999999 or ·9999999.

PB ■ 42

1 Correct questions are b, e and f.

2 *a* odd
b even
c even
d odd
e odd
f even
g even
h odd
i odd
j An odd number added to or
subtracted from an even number
always results in an odd number.
Two even or odd numbers added
or subtracted always results in an
even number.

3 385 + 198 = 583
385 − 198 = 187
385 + 346 = 731
385 − 346 = 39
385 + 281 = 666
385 − 281 = 104
198 + 346 = 544
346 − 198 = 148
198 + 281 = 479
281 − 198 = 83
346 + 281 = 627
346 − 281 = 65

(?) 385 + 198 + 346 = 929
385 + 198 + 281 = 864
385 + 346 + 281 = 1012
198 + 346 + 281 = 825
The sum of 2 odd numbers and 1
even number is even.
The sum of 2 even numbers and 1
odd number is odd.

PB ■ 43

1 a +
  b ×
  c ÷
  d −
  e ×, +
  f −, ÷

2 a Mon 625 km
    Tue 874 km
    Wed 788 km
    Thur 1500 km
  b Galina then Radek
  c 2459 km
  d 198 km

PB ■ 44

1 a 177
  b 531
  c 138
  d 414
  e 117
  f 945

2 a 24 Zoglans, 35 Zogglets
  b 16 Zoglans, 43 Zogglets

3 The answers are always odd
because when you add together an
odd number and an even number,
the total is odd.

(?) Whether the answer is odd or even
depends on how many odd numbers
there are in the sum. A single odd
number added to two even numbers
results in an odd number. Two odd
numbers added to an even number
results in an even number.

PB ■ 45

1 48p + £3·75 = £4·23
48p + £9·38+ £9·86
48p + 88p = £1·36
£3·75 + £9·38 = £13·13
£3·75 + 88p = £4·63
£9·38 + 88p = £10·26

2 a £11·52
  b £10·70
  c £3·85
  d £8·92
  e £8·10
  f £12·32
  g road atlas, flowers and chocolate
    bar
  h 10 litres of fuel, road atlas and
    sandwiches

PB ■ 46

1 a £115
  b £40
  c £24
  d 75
  e 75
  f 3·4

2 a 152, 608
  b 228, 532
  c 456, 304
  d 76, 684

PR ■ 47

1 a 160
  b 180
  c 300
  d 120
  e 490
  f 480

2 a Possible answers include: 2, 150;
    4, 300; 6, 450; 8, 600;
    10, 750; 12, 900
  b Possible answers include: 2, 60;
    4, 120; 6, 180; 8, 240;
    10, 300; 12, 360

3 Multiple answers are possible.

4 a $5 \times 9 \times 11$
  b Smallest: $5 \times 9 \times 11 = 495$,
    largest: $12 \times 11 \times 9 = 1188$
  c Smallest: $5 \times 6 \times 8 \times 9 = 2160$,
    largest: $8 \times 9 \times 11 \times 12 = 9504$

PB ■ 48

1 a 70
  b 64
  c 78
  d 132
  e 124
  f 81

2 a $3 \times 9 = 27$
    $9 \times 3 = 27$
    $27 \div 3 = 9$
    $27 \div 9 = 3$
    $9 + 9 + 9 = 27$
    $3 + 3 + 3 + 3 + 3 + 3 + 3 + 3$
      $+ 3 = 27$

b $4 \times 8 = 32$
    $8 \times 4 = 32$
    $32 \div 8 = 4$
    $32 \div 4 = 8$
    $8 + 8 + 8 + 8 = 32$
    $4 + 4 + 4 + 4 + 4 + 4 + 4$
      $+ 4 = 32$

3 $21 \times 3 = 63$, $3 \times 21 = 63$,
    $63 \div 3 = 21$, $63 \div 21 = 3$
    $63 \times 3 = 189$, $3 \times 63 = 189$,
    $189 \div 3 = 63$, $189 \div 63 = 3$
    $21 \times 7 = 147$, $7 \times 21 = 147$,
    $147 \div 21 = 7$, $147 \div 7 = 21$
    $63 \times 7 = 441$, $7 \times 63 = 441$,
    $441 \div 63 = 7$, $441 \div 7 = 63$
    $147 \times 3 = 441$, $3 \times 147 = 441$,
    $441 \div 3 = 147$, $441 \div 147 = 3$

PB ■ 49

1 a 60
  b 60
  c 66
  d 31
  e 16
  f 37
  g 40
  h 28

2 a

Input		Output 1
5	→	23
6	→	27
7	→	31
8	→	35
Input		Output 2
5	→	32
6	→	36
7	→	40
8	→	44

b The outputs are different
    because the machines perform
    different operations on the input
    numbers.

3 $(8 + 4) \times 2 = 24$
$(8 \times 4) + 2 = 34$
$8 + (4 \times 2) = 16$
$(2 \times 8) + 4 = 20$
$(8 + 2) \times 4 = 40$
$8 \times (4 + 2) = 48$

(?) $(8 - 2) \times 4 = 24,$
$8 \times (4 - 2) = 16,$
$(8 - 4) \times 2 = 8,$
$(4 \times 8) - 2 = 30$

PB ■ 50

1 a 12
b 7
c 11
d 8
e 24
f 19

2 a $18 \div 3 = 6$
b $28 \div 4 = 7, 28 \div 7 = 4$
c $72 \div 8 = 9$

3 $160 \div 4 = 40, 160 \div 40 = 4$
$40 \times 4 = 160, 8 \times 20 = 160$
$160 \div 8 = 20, 160 \div 20 = 8$
$160 \div 16 = 10, 160 \div 10 = 16$
$16 \times 10 = 160, 4 \times 20 = 80$
$80 \div 4 = 20, 80 \div 20 = 4$
$80 \div 8 = 10, 80 \div 10 = 8$
$8 \times 10 = 80, 4 \times 16 = 64$
$64 \div 4 = 16, 64 \div 16 = 4$
$40 \div 4 = 10, 40 \div 10 = 4$
$4 \times 10 = 40, 4 \times 8 = 32$
$32 \div 8 = 4, 32 \div 4 = 8$

(?) The multiplication answers would all
be 100 times bigger and the division
answers would stay the same. This
means there is no suitable 'card' to
complete any statement.

PB ■ 51

1 a 0·5
b $\frac{1}{4}$
c $\frac{1}{10}$
d $\frac{3}{4}$
e 0·3
f $\frac{7}{10}$

2 a £11·35
b £2·32
c £3·05

PB ■ 52

1 a 36
b 24
c 36
d 24
e 24
f 24
g 36
h 36
i 36
j 24
k 24
l 36

2

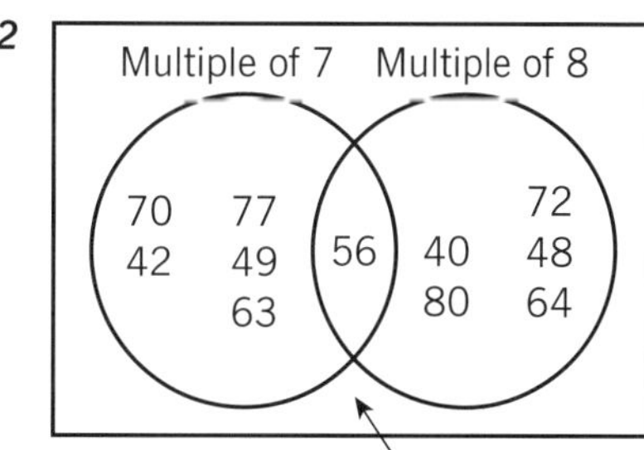

Any other number between
40 and 80 belongs to the
universal set.

3 a 40
b 42
c 36
d 24

PB ■ 53

1 a 39
  b 98
  c 48
  d 1340
  e 380
  f 1720
  g 4700
  h 13 000
  i 7300

2 a 19
  b 47
  c 17 400
  d £15 800
  e 36
  f 84

3 This can be done in many ways.
Encourage children to be
systematic.
$50 + 60 = 110$
$50 + 70 = 120$
$60 + 70 = 130$
$60 + 80 = 140$
$70 + 80 = 150$
$70 + 90 = 160$
$80 + 90 = 170$
$80 + 100 = 180$
$90 + 100 = 190$
There are many possible answers for
the relevant three multiples of ten.

(?) The patterns would be the same,
with each number 10 times greater.

PB ■ 54

1 a 7, 14, 28, 56, 112, 224
  b 13, 26, 52, 104, 208, 416
  c 25, 50, 100, 200, 400, 800

2 75, 150, 300, 600, 1200, 2400,
4800

3
$$100 \times 9 = 900 \qquad 6 \times 90 = 540$$
$$\downarrow \qquad \downarrow \qquad \downarrow \qquad \downarrow$$
$$50 \times 18 = 900 \qquad 12 \times 45 = 540$$
$$7 \times 70 = 490 \qquad 14 \times 25 = 350$$
$$\downarrow \qquad \downarrow \qquad \downarrow \qquad \downarrow$$
$$14 \times 35 = 490 \qquad 7 \times 50 = 350$$
$$35 \times 8 = 280 \qquad 15 \times 16 = 240$$
$$\downarrow \qquad \downarrow \qquad \downarrow \qquad \downarrow$$
$$70 \times 4 = 280 \qquad 30 \times 8 = 240$$

4

	$\times 6$	$\times 12$
$1 \times 3 = 3$	6	12
$2 \times 3 = 6$	12	24
$3 \times 3 = 9$	18	36
$4 \times 3 = 12$	24	48
$5 \times 3 = 15$	30	60
$6 \times 3 = 18$	36	72
$7 \times 3 = 21$	42	84
$8 \times 3 = 24$	48	96
$9 \times 3 = 27$	56	108
$10 \times 3 = 30$	60	120

PB ■ 55

1 a 1, 2, 4, 8, 16
  b 1, 2, 3, 6, 9, 18
  c 1, 2, 3, 4, 6, 8, 12, 24
  d 1, 2, 4, 8, 16, 32
  e 1, 2, 3, 4, 6, 9, 12, 18, 36

2 Possible answers include:
  a 2, 4, 6, 8, 10
  b 7, 14, 21, 28, 35, 42
  c 11, 22, 33, 44, 55, 66
  d 15, 30, 45, 60 75, 90
  e 4, 8, 12, 16, 20, 24
  f 56, 112, 168, 224, 280, 336
  g 12, 24, 36, 48, 60,72
  h 30, 60, 90,120,150,180

3 $7 \times 2 = 14$, $7 \times 3 = 21$,
$7 \times 5 = 35$, $5 \times 2 = 10$,
$5 \times 3 = 15$, $2 \times 3 = 6$ (numbers can
also be written in reverse order). On
some calculators entering a number
then pressing $\boxed{\times}$ $\boxed{=}$ produces the
square of that number. This facility
greatly increases the range of possible
answers.

? $7 \times 5 \times 3 = 105$, $7 \times 5 \times 2 = 70$,
$7 \times 3 \times 2 = 42$, $5 \times 2 \times 3 = 30$,
$2 \times 3 \times 5 \times 7 = 210$, $75 \times 3 = 225$,
$75 \times 2 = 150$, $75 \times 2 \times 3 = 450$,
$73 \times 5 = 365$, $73 \times 2 = 146$,
$73 \times 5 \times 2 = 730$, $72 \times 5 = 360$,
$72 \times 3 = 216$, $72 \times 5 \times 3 = 1080$,
$57 \times 3 = 171$, $57 \times 2 = 114$,
$57 \times 3 \times 2 = 342$, $53 \times 7 = 371$,
$53 \times 2 = 106$, $53 \times 7 \times 2 = 742$,
$52 \times 7 = 364$, $52 \times 3 = 156$,
$52 \times 7 \times 3 = 1092$, ...
(numbers can also be written in
reverse order)

PB ■ 56

1 *a* 150
  b 270
  c 440
  d 135
  e 243
  f 396
  g 165
  h 297
  i 484

2 *a* £5·33
  b £5·07

3 *a* £3·69
  b £3·51

4 Multiple answers are possible.
By finding the answer to $20 \times$ the
2-digit number first, $19 \times$ and
$21 \times$ the number can be found
through addition and subtraction.
The answer to $20 \times$ the 2-digit
number can be found by doubling
$10 \times$ the 2-digit number.

? Multiple answers are possible, but
related to $30 \times$ (or trebling $10 \times$)
the 2-digit number.

PB ■ 57

1 *a* 135
  b 124
  c 130
  d 182
  e 195
  f 228
  g 294
  h 368
  i 432

2 *a* £1·92
  b £2·96
  c £3·36
  d £2·24
  e £2·15

PB ■ 58

1 *a* 12
  b 12
  c 12
  d 6
  e 72
  f $\frac{1}{12}$

2 $\frac{1}{2}$ of $240 = 120$ $\frac{1}{2}$ of $120 = 60$
$\frac{1}{2}$ of $60 = 30$ $\frac{1}{3}$ of $240 = 80$
$\frac{1}{3}$ of $120 = 40$ $\frac{1}{3}$ of $60 = 20$
$\frac{1}{4}$ of $240 = 60$ $\frac{1}{4}$ of $120 = 30$
$\frac{1}{4}$ of $60 = 15$ $\frac{1}{5}$ of $240 = 48$
$\frac{1}{5}$ of $120 = 24$ $\frac{1}{5}$ of $60 = 12$
$\frac{1}{10}$ of $240 = 24$ $\frac{1}{10}$ of $120 = 12$
$\frac{1}{10}$ of $60 = 6$

3 $\frac{1}{3}$ of $24 = 8$, $\frac{1}{3}$ of $27 = 9$,
$\frac{1}{4}$ of $28 = 7$, $\frac{1}{4}$ of $32 = 8$,
$\frac{1}{4}$ of $36 = 9$, $\frac{2}{4}$ of $16 = 8$,
$\frac{2}{4}$ of $18 = 9$, $\frac{3}{4}$ of $12 = 9$,

$\frac{1}{6}$ of 42 = 7, $\frac{1}{6}$ of 54 = 9,

$\frac{2}{6}$ of 12 = 4, $\frac{3}{6}$ of 14 = 7,

$\frac{3}{6}$ of 18 = 9, $\frac{4}{6}$ of 12 = 8,

$\frac{1}{7}$ of 28 = 4, $\frac{1}{7}$ of 42 = 6,

$\frac{1}{7}$ of 56 = 8, $\frac{1}{7}$ of 63 = 9,

$\frac{2}{7}$ of 21 = 6, $\frac{3}{7}$ of 14 = 6,

$\frac{3}{7}$ of 21 = 9, $\frac{1}{8}$ of 24 = 3,

$\frac{1}{8}$ of 32 = 4, $\frac{1}{8}$ of 56 = 7,

$\frac{1}{8}$ of 72 = 9, $\frac{2}{8}$ of 16 = 4,

$\frac{2}{8}$ of 36 = 9, $\frac{3}{8}$ of 24 = 9,

$\frac{4}{8}$ of 12 = 6, $\frac{6}{8}$ of 12 = 9,

$\frac{1}{9}$ of 27 = 3, $\frac{1}{9}$ of 36 = 4,

$\frac{1}{9}$ of 54 = 6, $\frac{1}{9}$ of 63 = 7,

$\frac{1}{9}$ of 72 = 8, $\frac{2}{9}$ of 18 = 4,

$\frac{2}{9}$ of 36 = 8, $\frac{3}{9}$ of 12 = 4,

$\frac{3}{9}$ of 18 = 6, $\frac{3}{9}$ of 21 = 7,

$\frac{3}{9}$ of 24 = 8

PB ■ 59

1 *a* 360
  b 280
  c 560
  d 420
  e 2100
  f 2000
  g 6300
  h 7200

2 *a* 230
  b 138
  c 152
  d 329
  e 416
  f 486

3 *a* 948
  b 1325
  c 1944
  d 2464
  e 3216
  f 4842

PB ■ 60

1 *a* 565
  b 1268
  c 2844
  d 759
  e 2248
  f 4328

2 *a* 999

3 Largest answer: $876 \times 9 = 7884$, smallest answer: $234 \times 1 = 234$

(?) Largest answer: remains the same, smallest answer: 0

PB ■ 61

1 *a* 33·2
  b 29·6
  c 33
  d 36·5
  e 32·4
  f 53·6
  g 65·1
  h 48·5

2 *a* 3·3
  b 5·5
  c 7·7
  d 9·9

3 Product nearest to 50: $8·3 \times 6 = 49·8$, product furthest from 50: $2·3 \times 1 = 2·3$

(?) If the set of digits included 0 there would be more products available. The product nearest to 50 would remain the same but the product furthest from 50 would be 0, i.e. $1·2 \times 0 = 0$.

PB ■ 62

1 *a* 12, 120, 120, 1200
  b 40, 400, 400, 4000
  c 36, 360, 360, 3600

2 a 805
  b 1530
  c 2352
  d 1378
  e 2592
  f 3886
  g 3315
  h 5208

3 $23 \times 45 = 1035$, $24 \times 35 = 840$,
$25 \times 34 = 850$, $\quad 23 \times 54 = 1242$,
$24 \times 53 = 1272$, $25 \times 43 = 1075$,
$32 \times 45 = 1440$, $42 \times 35 = 1470$,
$52 \times 34 = 1768$, $32 \times 54 = 1728$,
$42 \times 53 = 2226$, $52 \times 43 = 2236$,
Numbers can also be written in reverse order.
Largest answer: 2236

(?) $234 \times 5 = 1170$, $245 \times 3 = 735$,
$235 \times 4 = 940$, $\quad 253 \times 4 = 1012$,
$243 \times 5 = 1215$, $254 \times 3 = 762$,
$345 \times 2 = 690$, $\quad 354 \times 2 = 708$,
$324 \times 5 = 1620$, $342 \times 5 = 1710$,
$325 \times 4 = 1300$, $352 \times 4 = 1408$,
$425 \times 3 = 1275$, $452 \times 3 = 1356$,
$435 \times 2 = 870$, $\quad 453 \times 2 = 906$,
$423 \times 5 = 2115$, $432 \times 5 = 2160$,
$523 \times 4 = 2092$, $534 \times 2 = 1068$,
$524 \times 3 = 1572$, $542 \times 3 = 1626$,
$532 \times 4 = 2128$, $543 \times 2 = 1086$,
Largest answer (2160) is smaller than the largest answer where the digits made two 2-digit numbers.

PB ■ 63

1 a 56
  b 87 r 1
  c 74
  d 61 r 5
  e 110 r 3
  f 81
  g 89 r 3
  h 94 r 4

2 a £0·56
  b £0·74
  c £8·10

3 There are 48 permutations. Of these, the following have remainders. The rest are whole number answers.

$206 \div 6 = 34 \text{ r } 2 \qquad 208 \div 6 = 34 \text{ r } 4$
$628 \div 6 = 104 \text{ r } 4 \quad 260 \div 6 = 43 \text{ r } 2$
$268 \div 6 = 44 \text{ r } 4 \qquad 640 \div 6 = 106 \text{ r } 4$
$602 \div 6 = 100 \text{ r } 2 \quad 280 \div 6 = 46 \text{ r } 4$
$682 \div 6 = 113 \text{ r } 4 \quad 608 \div 6 = 101 \text{ r } 2$
$286 \div 6 = 47 \text{ r } 4 \qquad 802 \div 6 = 133 \text{ r } 4$
$620 \div 6 = 103 \text{ r } 2 \quad 406 \div 6 = 67 \text{ r } 4$
$820 \div 6 = 136 \text{ r } 4 \quad 680 \div 6 = 113 \text{ r } 2$
$460 \div 6 = 76 \text{ r } 4 \qquad 826 \div 6 = 137 \text{ r } 4$
$806 \div 6 = 134 \text{ r } 2 \quad 604 \div 6 = 100 \text{ r } 4$
$862 \div 6 = 143 \text{ r } 4 \quad 860 \div 6 = 143 \text{ r } 2$
$284 \div 6 = 47 \text{ r } 2 \qquad 248 \div 6 = 41 \text{ r } 2$
$824 \div 6 = 137 \text{ r } 2 \quad 482 \div 6 = 80 \text{ r } 2$
$428 \div 6 = 71 \text{ r } 2 \qquad 842 \div 6 = 140 \text{ r } 2$

(?) All answers have remainders, which are all odd.

PB ■ 64

1 a 600
  b 500
  c 800
  d 750
  e 1000
  f 900
  g 1000
  h 1250

2 a 800, 756
  b 400, 456
  c 1000, 1056
  d 900, 928
  e 800, 984
  f 600, 576

3 1000   874
   1200   1197
   1200   1197
   1400   1428

4 Smallest: $18 \times 29 = 522$, largest: $91 \times 82 = 7462$

(?) Smallest: $289 \times 1 = 289$, largest: $821 \times 9 = 7389$

PB ■ 65

1 a 40 and 4
b 19 and 6

2 25

3 72

4 48

5 166

6 Possible answers include:
$4 \times 0 = 0$ $\quad$ $400 + 0 = 400$
Difference = 400
$4 \times 1 = 4$ $\quad$ $400 + 1 = 401$
Difference = 397
$4 \times 2 = 8$ $\quad$ $400 + 2 = 402$
Difference = 394
$4 \times 3 = 12$ $\quad$ $400 + 3 = 403$
Difference = 391
$4 \times 4 = 16$ $\quad$ $400 + 4 = 404$
Difference = 388
$4 \times 5 = 20$ $\quad$ $400 + 5 = 405$
Difference = 385
The difference descends in multiples of 3, so the difference is the least when:
$4 \times 133 = 532$ $\quad$ $400 + 133 = 533$
Difference = 1 $(400 \div 3 = 133 \cdot 333)$

(?) The difference descends in multiples of 1, so the difference is the least when:
$2 \times 200 = 400$ $\quad$ $200 + 200 = 400$
Difference = 0 $(200 \div 1 = 200)$

PB ■ 66

1 162p

2 Jacket £34, skirt £17

3 a 52p, 70p, 94p
b £1·30, £1·75, £2·35
c £6·76, £9·10, £12·22

4 £1·01, £1·06, £1·11, £1·16, £1·21, £1·26, £1·31, £1·36, £1·41, £1·46

5 £3·62

6 a £288 000
b £312 000
c £292 000

7 $1 \times 25p = 25p$
$(1 \times 25p) + (1 \times 35p) = 60p$
$(1 \times 25p) + (2 \times 35p) = 95p$
$(1 \times 25p) + (3 \times 35p) = £1·30$
$2 \times 25p = 50p$
$(2 \times 25p) + (1 \times 35p) = 85p$
$(2 \times 25p) + (2 \times 35p) = £1·20$
$(2 \times 25p) + (3 \times 35p) = £1·55$
$3 \times 25p = 75p$
$(3 \times 25p) + (1 \times 35p) = £1·10$
$(3 \times 25p) + (2 \times 35p) = £1·45$
$(3 \times 25p) + (3 \times 35p) = £1·80$
$4 \times 25p = £1$
$(4 \times 25p) + (1 \times 35p) = £1·35$
$(4 \times 25p) + (2 \times 35p) = £1·70$
$(4 \times 25p) + (3 \times 35p) = £2·05$
$1 \times 35p = 35p$
$2 \times 35p = 70p$
$3 \times 35p = £1.05$

PB ■ 67

1 a −
b ×
c ÷
d −
e ×, −
f ÷, +, =
g ×, ÷
h +, ÷

2 a 108
  b 36
  c 16
  d 32
  e 30
  f 6
  g 22
  h 38

PB ■ 68

1 a £1·20
  b £1·80
  c £3
  d £6
  e £10·20
  f £13·20

2 a $19·5, 2314 yen,
    31·2 Swiss francs
  b $54, 6408 yen,
    86·4 Swiss francs
  c $8·25, 979 yen,
    13·2 Swiss francs
  d $10·95, 1299·4 yen,
    17·52 Swiss francs
  e $10·2, 1210·4 yen,
    16·32 Swiss francs
  f $17·1, 2029·2 yen,
    27·36 Swiss francs

3 a 2225 yen
  b £12·50

4 a $15
  b £10

PB ■ 69

1 a 2300 m
  b 5500 m
  c 10 100 m
  d 15 800 m
  e 700 m
  f 900 m
  g 3250 m
  h 7750 m

2 a 300 mm, **30 cm**, **0·3 m**
  b **800 mm**, 80 cm, **0·8 m**
  c **400 mm**, **40 cm**, 0·4 m
  d 700 mm, **70 cm**, **0·7 m**
  e **750 mm**, 75 cm, **0·75 m**
  f **100 mm**, **10 cm**, 0·1 m

3 a 1   2   3   **4**   5   **6** miles
    1·6 3·2 **4·8 6·4** **8** 9·6 km
  b 80 km, 20 miles, 100 miles

4

Number of lines	Total length of lines
4	50 mm
5	75 mm
6	105 mm
7	140 mm
8	180 mm
9	225 mm
10	275 mm
11	330 mm
12	390 mm
13	455 mm

PB ■ 70

1 a 23 mm
  b 48 mm
  c 67 mm
  d 88 mm

2 a 1 cm
  b 6 cm
  c 9 cm

3 1.3 m

4 a 600 cm, 592 cm
  b 990 cm, 988 cm
  c 1330 cm, 1326 cm
  d 1170 cm, 1171 cm

5 *a* between 4995 mm and 5004 mm
  b between 505 cm and 514 cm
  c between 5·5 m and 6·4 m

PB ■ 71

1

Bounce	Calculator keys	Height
1	500 × 40%	200 m
2	200 × 40%	80 m
3	80 × 40%	32 m
4	32 × 40%	12·8 m
5	13 × 40%	5·1 m
6	5 × 40%	2 m
7	2 × 40%	0·8 m
8	1 × 40%	0·4 m

If child does not clear each display,
and simply keeps keying ×40%,
the last display will be 0·3 (to the
nearest tenth).

2 After 7th bounce

(?) He will rise less than 1 m after the
7th bounce.

PB ■ 72

1

	1000 g	500 g	200 g	100 g	50 g
peaches 3250 g	3	–	1	–	1
bananas 4700 g	4	1	1	–	–
oranges 5300 g	5	–	1	1	–
pears 6450 g	6	–	2	–	1

2 Brie 630 g, Edam 970 g,
Cheddar 770 g, Parmesan 2190 g,
Stilton 1680 g

3 *a* 90 g
  b 90 g

PB ■ 73

1 *a* 3500 ml
  b 5250 ml
  c 2100 ml
  d 4750 ml
  e 6500 ml
  f 8700 ml
  g 2010 ml
  h 4060 ml
  i 750 ml
  j 7200 ml
  k 9330 ml
  l 9600 ml

2 *a* 600 ml, 250 ml, 1320 ml,
    500 ml, 3 l, 6 l
  b 2.5 l, 25 l
  c 48 l, 480 l

3 *a*

4 l jug	7 l jug	large	
4	0	0	fill 4 l jug
0	0	4	transfer to large
4	0	4	fill 4 l jug
0	0	8	transfer to large
0	7	1	transfer to 7 l jug

b

4 l jug	7 l jug	large	
4	0	0	fill 4 l jug
0	4	0	transfer to 7 l jug
4	0	0	fill 4 l jug
1	7	0	transfer to 7 l jug
0	7	1	transfer to 1 l jug
Repeat above processs.			

Other ways are posssible.

PB ■ 74

1 *a* 150 ml
   b 220 ml
   c 140 ml
   d 50 ml

2 *a* 15 l
   b 70 l
   c 40 l

3 5·25 l

4 4000 l

5
3 litres	3
4 litres	7 − 3
5 litres	12 − 7
6 litres	12 − 3 − 3
7 litres	7
8 litres	12 − 7 + 3
9 litres	12 − 3
10 litres	7 + 3

PB ■ 75

1

pints	ml	l
1	570	0·57
2	1140	1·14
4	2280	2·28
8	4560	4·56
10	5700	5·7

2 *a* >
   b >
   c ≈
   d <
   e <
   f <
   g >
   h <

3 *a* McDonalds, 300 ml
   b 5 weeks
   c 4 weeks

PB ■ 76

1 *a*

black	purple	blue	grey
1	3	5	7
4	12	20	28

   b

black	purple	blue	grey
1	2	3	4
6	12	18	24

2 *a* square

1	2	3	4	5	6

Length of a side in cm

1·1	1·5	2·1	3	4·2	6

Perimeter in cm

4·4	6	8·4	12	16·8	24

   b Children may notice that the length of side of alternate squares appears to double.

PB ■ 77

1 *a* 8 cm^2
   b 9 cm^2
   c 20 cm^2

2 *a* 20 cm, 22 cm, 28 cm or 50 cm
   b Possible answers include: 11 cm^2, 20 cm^2, 27 cm^2, 32 cm^2, 35 cm^2, 36 cm^2

3 *a* 1800 cm^2
   b 2400 cm^2
   c 150 cm^2
   d 900 cm^2
   e 1000 cm^2

4 c, d, e, a, b

PB ■ 78

1 *A* 7:25/07:25
   B 11:05/23:05
   C 6:20/06:20
   D 6:40/18:40

E 3:55/15:55
F 12:05/12:05
G 2:50/02:50
H 12:30/00:30

2 *a* 00:30, 02:50, 06:30, 08:00, 10:30, 12:05, 20:00, 21:30
b 9 hr 30 min
c 15 hours
d 15:00

PB ■ 79

1 *a* 08:00, 08:10, 08:20, 08:30, 08:40, 08:50, 09:00, 09:10
b 08:00, 08:12, 08:24, 08:36, 08:48, 09:00, 09:12, 09:24
c 08:00, 08:20, 08:40, 09:00, 09:20, 09:40, 10:00, 10:20

2 09:00

3 14:00

PB ■ 80

1 CFR, FRC, RCF, CRF, FCR, RFC

2 PFCN, FCNP, CNPF, NPFC, PCFN, CFNP, FNPC, NPCF, PNFC, NFCP, FCPN, CPNF, PCNF, CNFP, NFPC, FPCN, PNCF, NCFP, CFPN, FPNC, PFNC, FNCP, NCPF, CPFN

Possible answers include:

	P	*F*	*C*	*N*
Breakfast	7.00	7.45	8.30	9.15
Lunch	11.45	12.30	1.15	2.00
Dinner	6.00	6.45	7.30	8.15

PB ■ 81

1 Pentominoes d, f, i and j do not make open cubes.

It is then possible to make nets for complete cubes.

PB ■ 82

1 By following the instructions, each child makes a tetrahedron.

a Yes
b Diagonal:width = 2:1

PB ■ 83

1 Perpendicular: c, g
parallel: a, b, d, e, f, h

2 AB // CD, AC // BD, AB ⊥ BD, AC ⊥ AB

PB ■ 84

1

Saucer	Distance	Flight path
Beta	6000	70°
Charlie	8000	70°
Delta	7000	40°
Echo	2000	80°
Foxtrot	5000	50°
Gamma	4000	30°
Inca	5000	0°
Lima	1000	30°
Peru	6000	90°

2 Lima, Echo, Alpha, Gamma, Foxtrot and Inca, Beta and Peru, Delta, Charlie

3 Saucer Quito: 5 s miles, 6 s miles or 7 s miles from base

PB ■ 85

1

angle	a	b	c	d	e	f	g	h
size	40°	90°	25°	65°	75°	10°	150°	140°

2 *a* 60°, 60°, 60°
  b 70°, 70°, 110°, 110°
  c 55°, 55°, 125°, 125°
  d 60°, 60°, 120°, 120°
  e 35°, 35°, 110°

3 Total of angles in all triangles is 180° and of angles in quadrilaterals is 360°.

PB ■ 86

1 Child's own work.

2 *a* 65°
  b 54°
  c 6°
  d 95°
  e 65°
  f 103°

3 *a* 45° acute
  b 90° right angle
  c 135° obtuse
  d 180° straight angle
  e 90° right angle
  f 180° straight angle
  g 45° acute
  h 135° obtuse
  i 135° obtuse

4 *a* 30° acute
  b 60° acute
  c 90° right angle
  d 150° obtuse
  e 120° obtuse
  f 180° straight angle

PB ■ 87

1 100, 50, 50, 10, 10, 9, 8

PB ■ 88

1 *a* 50p
  b 22p
  c 60p
  d £3
  e £18
  f £1·80
  g £15
  h £1·15
  i £1
  j £2·40
  k £8·50
  l £78

2 a and d are false

3 Possible answers include:
£2 + 50p
£2 + 20p + 20p + 10p
£2 + 20p + (3 × 10p)
£2 + (5 × 10p)
£1 + £1 + 50p
£1 + £1 + 20p + 20p + 10p
£1 + £1 + 20p + (3 × 10p)
(5 × 50p)
£1 + (3 × 50p)
£1 + (2 × 50p) + (2 × 20p) + 10p

? Possible answers include:
£2 + £1
£2 + (2 × 50p)
£2 + 50p + (2 × 20p) + 10p
£1 + £1 + 50p + 50p
£1 + £1 + 50p + (2 × 20p) + 10p
£1 + (4 × 50p)
(6 × 50p)

PB ■ 89

1

11	1
12	0
13	0
14	0
15	3
16	5
17	10
18	6
19	5
20	2

2 *a* 4

  b 23

  c Easy because most of the children scored 17 or more

  d 17

(?) Possible answers include:

  a How many children scored 16?

  b How many children scored between 12 and 14?

  c How many children scored 14 or less?

PB ■ 90

1 *a* True

  b False

  c True. It could be in the 'Other' category

  d False. The graph does not provide information about how often or in what quantities the fruits are eaten.

2 Child's own work. The table should have a frequency of around 8 for each number and total of frequencies 50.

3 Child's own work. The bar line chart must have a title and labels for both axes.

(?) There is likely to be less variation in frequency, which will be around 17 for each number.

PB ■ 91

1 *a* Amy

  b Rob

  c Jan and March

  d between Feb and March

  e about £20

  f about £34

(?) Child's own graph. This needs to show Rob saving money at a steady rate, averaging around £40 a month.

PB ■ 92

1 Child's own work.

2 Child's own work.

(?) If the results from questions 1 and 2 are similar, they are likely to give a good prediction.

ACTIVITY SHEETS

AS ■ 1

1 *a* hundreds
    b thousands
    c ten thousands
    d hundred thousands
    e ten thousands
    f millions

2 *a* 875 432
    b 234 578
    c 437 258, 437 285, 437 528,
       437 582, 437 825 or 437 852;
       324 578, 324 587, 324 758,
       324 785, 324 857 or 324 875;
       823 574, 832 547, 823 457 or
       823 475

3 599 910, 599 920, 599 930,
    599 940, 599 950, 599 960,
    599 970, 599 980, 599 990,
    600 010

AS ■ 2

1 *a* 3552, 3542, 4542
    b 5974, 4974, 5074
    c 6103, 6003, 5003

2 Child's own work.

AS ■ 3

1 3·3, 6·2, 6·3, 6·9, 7·4

2 3·52 m, 2·04 m, 1·91 m, 1·69 m,
    1·65 m

3 *a* 9·86
    b 3·68
    c 3·68
    d 9·86
    e 6·83, 6·89

AS ■ 4

1 *a* 6400
    b 4800
    c 8300
    d 3900
    e 5000
    f 8000

2 *a* 3300 + 1200 = 4500
    b 3500 + 3400 = 6900
    c 4800 + 7100 = 11 900
    d 4501, 6877, 11 995

3 *a* between 3675 and 3684
    b between 7850 and 7949
    c between 8500 and 9499

4 150, 151, 152, 153, 154
    150 rounded to the nearest 10:
    between 145 and 154,
    200 rounded to the nearest 100:
    between 150 and 249

The numbers would be between
155 and 164

AS ■ 5

1 *a* −1, −5, −9
    b −2, −5, −8
    c 1, −4, −9
    d −5, 0, 5

2 *a* −5, −1, 6, 7
    b −8, 0, 7, 9
    c −20, −9, 0, 15
    d −12, −9, −5, −4

3 Multiple answers are possible:
    −9 or −8 in each 1st circle,
    −6, −5, −4, −3 in each 2nd circle,
    −1 or 0 in each last circle.

AS ■ 6

1 a 12, 18, 24, 30, 36, 42, 48, 54, 60
  b 14, 21, 28, 35, 42, 49, 56, 63, 70
  c 16, 24, 32, 40, 48, 56, 64, 72, 80
  d 18, 27, 36, 45, 54, 63, 72, 81, 90
  e Child's own work.
  f Child's own work. The numbers increase in column 1 by 1, in column 2 by 2, …

2 Grids might be: $3 \times 4 = 12$,
  $3 \times 6 = 18$, $3 \times 7 = 21$,
  $3 \times 8 = 24$, $3 \times 9 = 27$,
  $4 \times 6 = 24$, $4 \times 7 = 28$,
  $4 \times 8 = 32$, $4 \times 9 = 36$,
  $6 \times 7 = 42$, $6 \times 8 = 48$,
  $6 \times 9 = 54$, $7 \times 8 = 56$,
  $7 \times 9 = 63$, $8 \times 9 = 72$

AS ■ 7

1 a All even numbers are crossed and numbers that end in a 5 or 0 are ringed. Therefore numbers that end in 0 are both ringed and crossed.
  b The numbers are all multiples of 10.

2 Multiples of 3: 3 9 15 21 27 33 39 45,
  Intersection: 6 12 18 24 30 36 42 48,
  Multiples of 2: 2 4 8 10 14 16 20 22 26 28 32 34 38 40 44 46 50,
  Outside diagram: 0 1 5 7 11 13 17 19 23 25 29 31 35 37 41 43 47 49.
  Numbers in the overlap are multiples of 6.

AS ■ 8

1 $1^2 = 1$, $2^2 = 4$, $3^2 = 9$, $4^2 = 16$,
  $5^2 = 25$, $6^2 = 36$, $7^2 = 49$,
  $8^2 = 64$, $9^2 = 81$, $10^2 = 100$

2 a Square number: 1, 4, 9, 16, 25, 36, 49, 64, 81, 100, unit digit: 1, 4, 9, 6, 5, 6, 9, 4, 1, 0
  b There is a symmetrical pattern: the numbers either side of 5 are the same.

3 a 169, 196, 225, 256, 289, 324, 361, 400
  b There is a repeating pattern, continuing from that shown in 2a: 1, 4, 9, 6, 5, 6, 9, 4, 1, 0 …

AS ■ 9

1 Child's own work.

2 a False
  b True
  c True
  d False
  e Child's own work.

AS ■ 10

Fraction game for 2.

AS ■ 11

1 a £25
  b 51
  c $\frac{1}{100}$
  d Possible answers include: $\frac{1}{2}$ of 80 = 40, $\frac{1}{4}$ of 80 = 20

AS ■ 12

Decimal game for 2.

AS ■ 13

Fractions and decimals snap.

AS ■ 14

Percentages jigsaw.

AS ■ 15

Equivalent fractions, decimals and percentages: game.

AS ■ 16

1 **a** 6296
  b 1936
  c 1854
  d 3253

2 **a** 400
  b 90
  c 40
  d 600

3 One possible journey:
$2000 \to +1 \to 2001 \to -100 \to$
$1901 \to -10 \to 1891 \to +1000$
$\to 2891 \to -1 \to 2890 \to +10$
$\to 2900 \to -1000 \to 1900 \to$
$+100 \to 2000$

AS ■ 17

1 **a** Ticked answers are:
$710 - 140 = 570,$
$710 - 570 = 140,$
$140 + 570 = 710$
  b $701 + 140 = 841,$
$140 - 701 = -561,$
$140 + 701 = 841,$
$570 - 701 = -131,$
$570 - 701 = 1271,$
$701 + 570 = 1271$

2 Possible trails include:
$71 -17 +27 -10 +36 -46 = 61$
$71 +54 -54 -16 +16 +42 +36$
  $-46 = 103$
$71 +54 -44 +17 +16 -32 -46$
  $= 36$
$71 -17 +27 -10 +42 -32 -46$
  $= 35$
  a $71 - 17 + 17 + 16 + 42 + 36$
    $- 46 = 119$
  or, $71 + 54 - 54 + 16 + 42 +$
  $36 - 46 = 119$
  b $71 - 17 + 17 + 16 - 32 - 46 = 9$

AS ■ 18

1

	a	**b**	**c**
	3624	7369	4835
	+ 3872	+ 2413	+ 1437
	7496	9782	6272

2 **a** 587, 578, 875, 857, 758, 785

b + c

587	587	587
578	578	578
875	857	758
2040	2022	1923
587	587	587
578	875	875
785	857	758
1950	2319	2220
587	587	587
875	857	857
785	758	785
2247	2202	2229
578	578	578
875	875	875
857	758	785
2310	2211	2238
578	578	875
857	857	857
758	785	758
2193	2220	2490
875	857	758
857	758	785
785	785	578
2517	2400	2121
758	758	
785	785	
587	875	
2130	2418	

d totals, from smallest to largest:
1923, 1950, 2022, 2040, 2121,
2130, 2193, 2202, 2211, 2220,
2229, 2238, 2247, 2310, 2319,
2400, 2418, 2490, 2517;
differences: 27, 72, 18, 81, 9, 63,
9, 9, 9, 9, 9, 9, 63, 9, 18, 72, 27

e They are all divisible by 3.

AS ■ 19

1 a £37·45 b £40·63 c £64·77
  + £8·47 + £16·54 + £2·86
  —————— —————— ——————
  £45·92   £57·17   £67·63

2 a

12 7	1C	28 7
19·3	69·7	89
32	85·7	117·7

b

2·64	7·41	8·22	18·27
3·67	9·81	4·58	18·06
8·97	1·29	6·75	17·01
15·28	18·51	19·55	53·34

3 Multiple answers are possible.

4 Possible answers include:
  a 12·3 + 45·6 + 78·9
  b 94·1 + 85.2 + 76·3
  c 61·8 + 57·2 + 43·9
  d 78·3 + 69·2 + 54·1

AS ■ 20

1 a   8639 b   9712 c   5264
    − 4873   − 4339   − 1839
    —————— —————— ——————
      3766   5373   3425

2 a 4658
  b 651
  c 3072
  d 10 921
  Message is 'What has five sides?'

3 Child's own subtractions with answers 9516, 3518, 4016 and 6572.

4 Multiple answers are possible.

AS ■ 21

1 a   35·8 b   47·63 c   62·47
    − 8·4   − 16·56   − 39·84
    —————— —————— ——————
    27·4   31·07   22·63

2 a 9·7   1·2   6·7
      8·5   5·5
        3
  b 7·7   1·1   9·4   1·8
      6·6   8·3   7·6
        1·7   0·7
          1
  c 9·7   2·1   1·7   3·8
      1·2   0·4   2·1
        0·8   1·7
          0·9

3 5·21 m, 5·54 m, 8·69 m, 12·35 m

4 £8·07, £15·51, £11·52, £6·14

AS ■ 22

1 a £6.77
  b £6.67
  c £6.57

2 Possible answers include:
  a 26 = 67 − 34 − 7
  b 513 = 67 + 446
  c 79 = 36 + 36 + 7
  d 111 = 77 + 34

3 a 10p + 40p + 80p + £3·20
     + £6·40
  b 20p + 80p + £6·40 + £25·60
     + £51·20
  c Child's own work.

AS ■ 23

1 a tick
  b cross
  c tick
  d tick
  e cross
  f cross

2 a even, even, odd
  b even, odd, odd
  c even, even, odd
  d even, odd, odd

AS ■ 24

1 *a* 9·55 m
   b 2·150 l
   c £4·14
   d 50p, 5p, 1p

2 Star System Modia: The centre number is always 9 more than start number. Star System Shok: The centre number is always 4
   c 47

Child's own work.

AS ■ 25

1 *a* 9·6 cm
   b 10·2 cm

2 *a* 135
   b 128
   c 118
   d 122
   e 253
   f 250
   g 3
   h 503

3

Day 1	2	3	4	5	6	7	8
2	5	8	11	14	17	20	23

AS ■ 26

1 *a* £2
   b £1

2 *a* 15p
   b 30p

3 *a* 4p, 8p, 16p, 32p, 64p; less than £5. Total for week = £1·27
   b £1·28, £2·56, £5·12, £10·24, £20·48, £40·96, £81·92; more than £20.
   Total for 2 weeks = £162·56

4 5p, 10p, 20p, 40p, 80p, £1·60, £3·20 = £6·35

5 Multiple answers are possible. The 5 prices should total £5.

AS ■ 27

1 *a* 20, 40
   b 7, 14
   c 11, 77

AS ■ 28

1 *a* Joined to 1: 17, 25, 41, 49
   Joined to 2: 22, 26, 38,
   Joined to 3: 23, 27, 31, 35, 39
   b Multiple answers are possible.

2 4 r 2, $4\frac{1}{2}$
   5 r 1, $5\frac{1}{5}$
   6 r 3, $6\frac{3}{5}$
   1 r 7, $1\frac{7}{10}$

3 *a* circle 5, 9, 17, 29, 41, 45; cross 5, 17, 23, 26, 29, 41
   b Possible answers include: 53, 65, 77, 89, 101
   c 5, 17, 29, 41
   d They are all prime numbers. Each is 12 greater than the number before.

AS ■ 29

1 $0·5 = \frac{1}{2}$, $0·25 = \frac{1}{4}$, $0·75 = \frac{3}{4}$, $0·1 = \frac{1}{10}$, $0·2 = \frac{1}{5}$, $0·3 = \frac{3}{10}$

2

9 r 1	$9\frac{1}{2}$	9·5
12 r 1	$12\frac{1}{2}$	12·5
6 r 2	$6\frac{1}{2}$	6·5
7 r 2	$7\frac{1}{2}$	7·5
7 r 1	$7\frac{1}{5}$	7·2
8 r 1	$8\frac{1}{5}$	8·2
5 r 1	$5\frac{1}{10}$	5·1
6 r 7	$6\frac{7}{10}$	6·7

AS ■ 30

1 6

2 6 each, 5 are left.

3 7

4 6 each, 2 are left.

5 £6·50

6 £6·50

7 6·75 kg

8 6·5 cm

9 6·5 litres

10 6·75 cm

11 7

12 6

13 6p in each pile, 2p left over.

14 6p each, 5p left.

AS ■ 31

1 *a* 9
  b 4
  c 7
  d 36
  e 3
  f 7

2 *a* 36 ÷ 6 = 6, 48 ÷ 8 = 6,
    42 ÷ 7 = 6
  b 56 ÷ 8 = 7, 49 ÷ 7 = 7,
    42 ÷ 6 = 7
  c 56 ÷ 7 = 8, 48 ÷ 6 = 8,
    64 ÷ 8 = 8
  d 72 ÷ 8 = 9, 63 ÷ 7 = 9,
    81 ÷ 9 = 9
  e 72 ÷ 9 = 8, 64 ÷ 8 = 8,
    56 ÷ 7 = 8
  f 49 ÷ 7 = 7, 63 ÷ 9 = 7,
    56 ÷ 8 = 7

AS ■ 32

1 & 2

a	1200	R	*b*	360	P
c	270	E	*d*	270	E
e	370	C	*f*	1200	R
g	150	T	*h*	3600	I
i	100	A	*j*	5	M
k	700	N	*l*	270	E
m	56	G	*n*	150	T
o	3000	L	*p*	270	E
q	270	E	*r*	1200	R

AS ■ 33

1 *a* 172
  b 75
  c 312
  d 127
  e 217
  f 195

1	6	6	3	5	1
2	0	1	8	1	7
6	3	2	4	9	2
2	1	7	5	5	9

2 Possible answers include:
  75 ÷ 1, 150 ÷ 2, 225 ÷ 3,
  300 ÷ 4, 375 ÷ 5, 450 ÷ 6,
  525 ÷ 7, 600 ÷ 8, 675 ÷ 9,
  750 ÷ 10, 825 ÷ 11, 900 ÷ 12,
  975 ÷ 13, 1050 ÷ 14

AS ■ 34

1 *a* heart beat over a minute
  b a × 60
  c b × 24
  d c × 7
  e d × 52

2 a 29×30
  b 58×59
  c 76×77
  d 91×92

3 The number will always end with the digit 3 and the first two digits are the number first thought of.

AS ■ 35

1 b

Spaceship	Length of line	
to Alpha	34 mm	3·4 cm
to Bravo	49 mm	4·9 cm
to Charlie	73 mm	7·3 cm
to Delta	77 mm	7·7 cm
to Echo	62 mm	6·2 cm
to Foxtrot	40 mm	4·0 cm

2

Star	A	B	C	D
Perimeter (in mm)	210	320	430	540

c The perimeter of each star is 10 times the length of one side, and is 110 mm longer than the next smaller star.

AS ■ 36

1

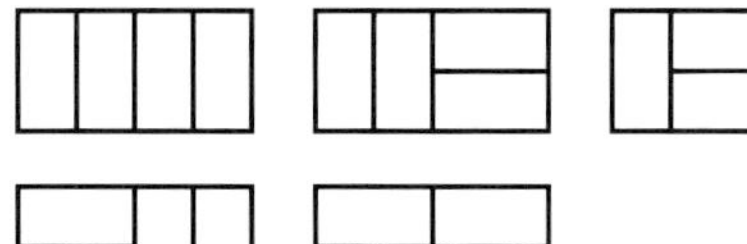

2 True

Length of walkways	1 m	2 m	3 m	4 m	5 m	6 m
Number of ways	1	2	3	5	8	13

The next number is the sum of the previous two numbers.

AS ■ 37

1 Samples – mass in kg

	1	2	3	4	5	6
a	6·4	6·7	6·8	7·1	7·3	7·6
b	6	7	7	7	7	7

c 42 kg
d 41·9 kg

2 a A 100 g, B 100 g, C 200 g, D 300 g
  b 200 g
  c 180 g

3 250 g, 260 g, 270 g, 280 g, 290 g, 300 g, 310 g, 320 g, 330 g, 340 g

AS ■ 38

a 7 trips
  one example:

Trip	Planet	Transporter	Flying saucer
1	Rah Baj	→ Yot (45z) Gri (40z)	Gri Yot
2	Rah Baj Yot	← Yot (45z)	Gri
3	Baj Yot	→ Rah (70z)	Rah Gri
4	Gri Bah Yot	← Gri (40z)	Rah
5	Baj	→ Gri (40z) Yot(45)	Rah Gri Yot
6	Baj Gri	← Gri (40z)	Rah Yot
7		→ Baj (60z) Gr(40z)	Rah Baj Yot Gri

b Trip 3 of this journey plan.

ACTIVITY SHEETS

AS ■ 39

1 a $5 \times 1, 6 \times 1, 7 \times 1$
  b 6 cm, 8 cm, 10 cm, 12 cm, 14 cm, 16 cm
  c 44 cm

2 a 10·5 cm
  b 12 cm
  c 10·5 cm
  d 9 cm
  e 10·5 cm
  f 12 cm

AS ■ 40

1 a 8 cm², 16 cm
  b 7 cm², 12 cm
  c 12 cm², 16 cm

2 Child's own work.

3 Squares of side 2 cm, 3 cm and 4 cm.

AS ■ 41

1 a

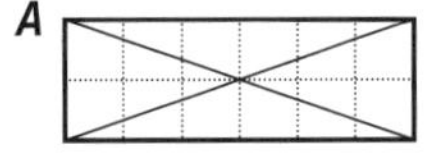

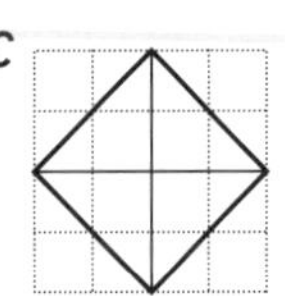
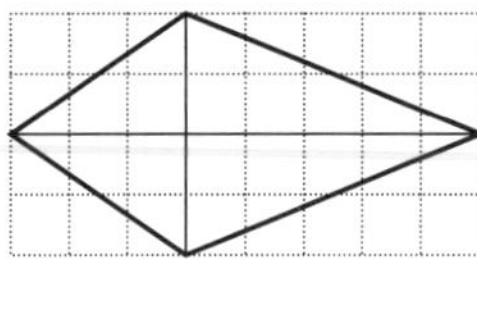

b

Property	A	B	C
All angles are right angles	✓	✗	✓
Opposite sides are equal	✓	✗	✓
Opposite sides are parallel	✓	✗	✓
Has 2 lines of symmetry	✓	✗	✓
Diagonals are equal	✓	✗	✓
Diagonals cross at rt angles	✗	✓	✓

2 b 1 square
  11 rectangles (since the square is a special rectangle)
  20 right angles

3

Number of wall tiles	4	5	6
No of rectangles	10	15	21

AS ■ 42

1 Child's own work

2

Triangle	Equal sides	Equal angles	Lines of symmetry	Name
a	2	2	1	isosceles
b	3	3	3	equilateral
c	0	0	0	scalene
d	0	0	0	scalene
e	Child's own work.			
f	Child's own work.			
g	Child's own work.			
h	Child's own work.			

? You couldn't draw an equilateral triangle.

AS ■ 43

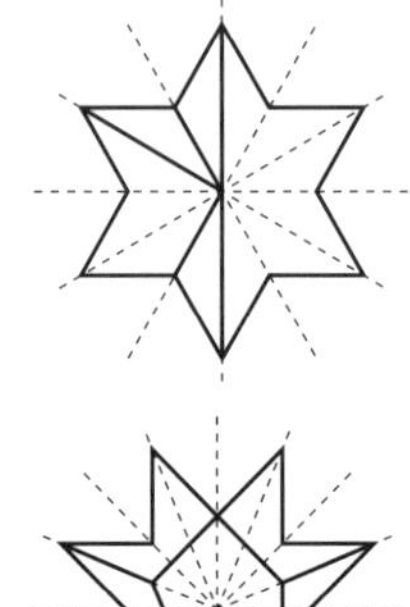
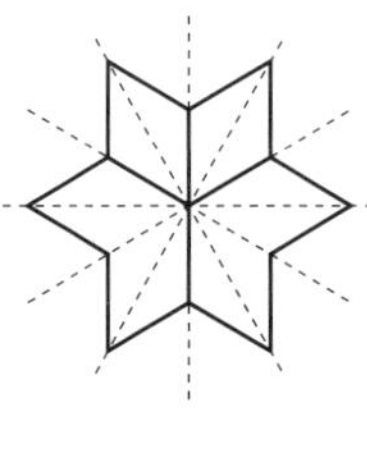

AS ■ 44

1 a

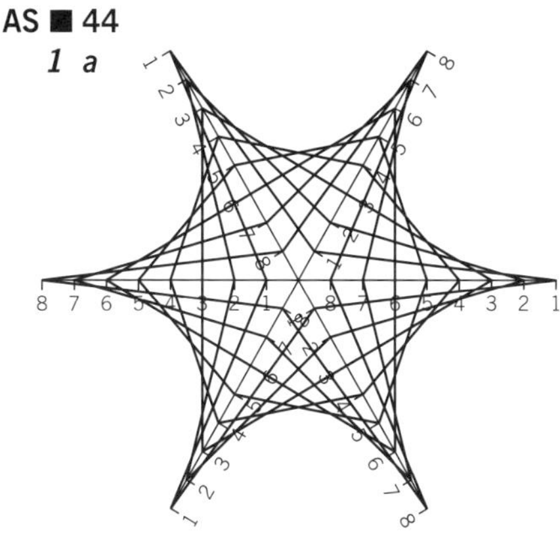

b equilateral triangles

AS ■ 45

1 Child's own work.

has line symmetry

has 3 colours

9

2

8

4 5 7

10

1

3

6

contains a ◇ shape

a Shapes 2 and 8
b Shape 2
c Shape 6

Ensure 3 different, yet overlapping, criteria are used.

AS ■ 46

1 & 2

Regular Polygon	Number of		
	equal sides	equal angles	axes of symmetry
Equilateral triangle	3	3	3
Square	4	4	4
Pentagon	5	5	5
Hexagon	6	6	6
Octagon	8	8	8
7-sided	7	7	7
9-sided	9	9	9
10-sided	10	10	10
12-sided	12	12	12

AS ■ 47

1 a

	R			R	
R	B			B	R
R	B			B	R
	R			R	

b

	G			G	
	R			R	
Y		R	R		Y
Y		R	R		Y
	R			R	
	G			G	

c

		B	B		
G	R	Y	Y	R	G
G	R	Y	Y	R	G
		B	B		

2 *a* *b* *e* *f*

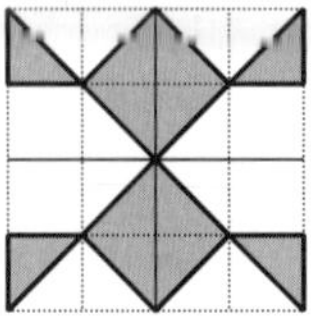

c *d*

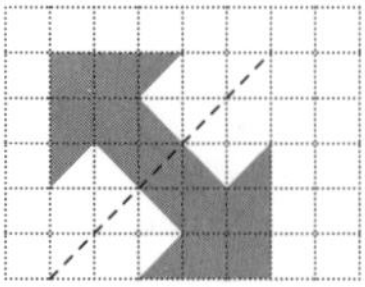

2 *a*

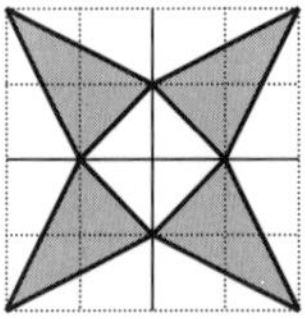

b

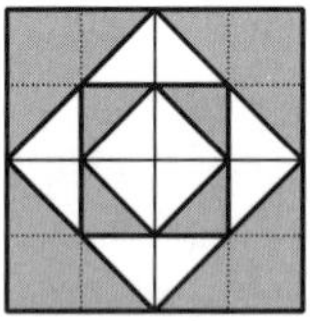

c

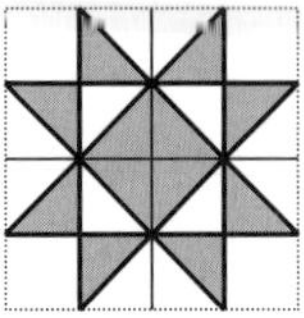

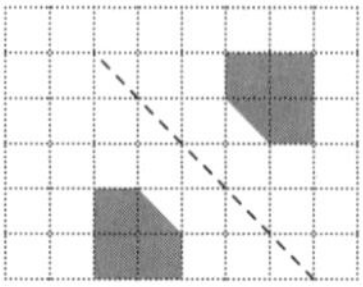

3

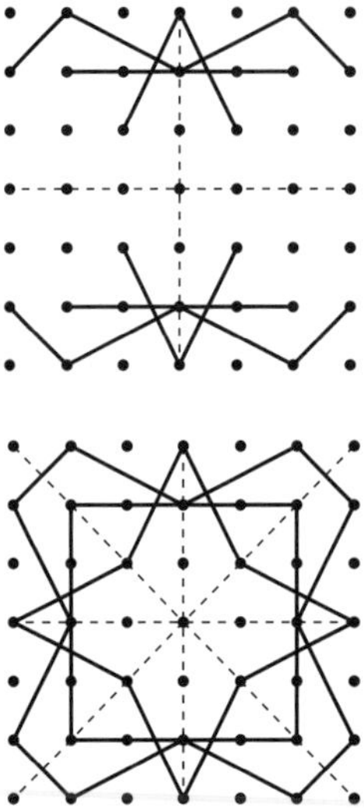

AS ■ 48

1 *a* *b*

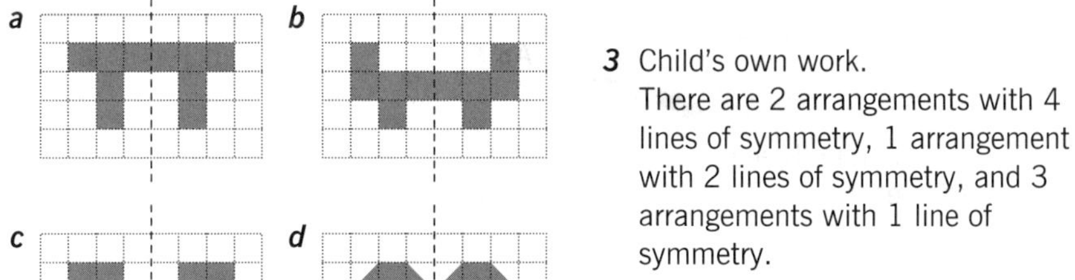

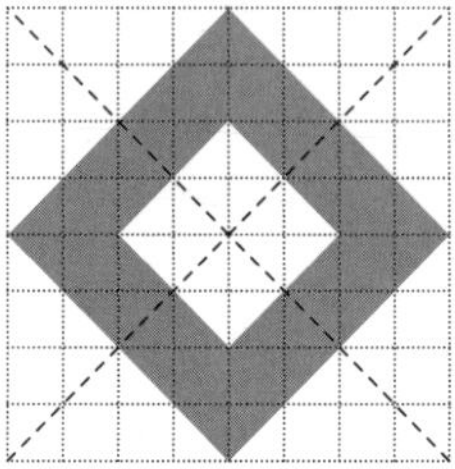

c 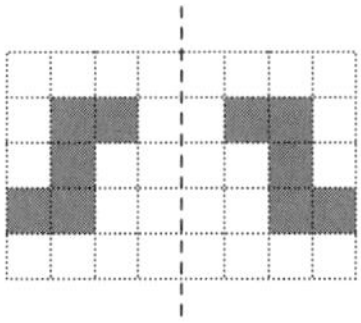 *d*

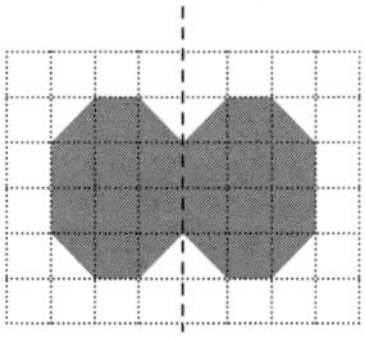

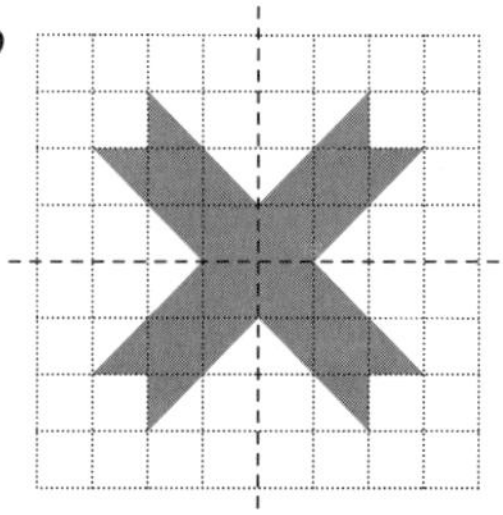

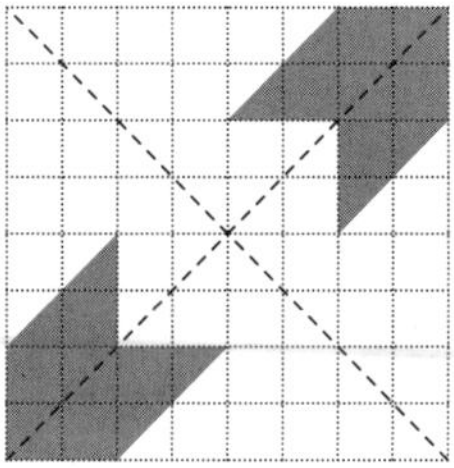

3 Child's own work.
There are 2 arrangements with 4 lines of symmetry, 1 arrangement with 2 lines of symmetry, and 3 arrangements with 1 line of symmetry.

1

a

b

c

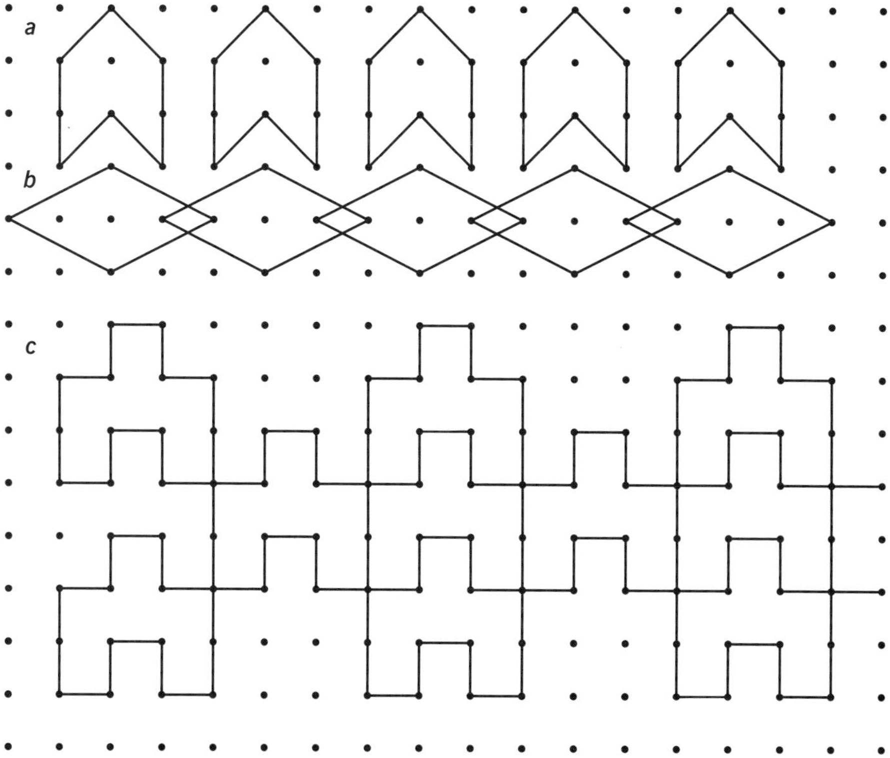

2 Possible answers include:

More or less than three colours may be used in each case.

AS ■ 50

1 a A (6, 10) and C (6, 1)
b E (1, 6) and G (10, 6)
c B (0, 3)
d F (3, 0)
e D (9, 9)

2 heptagon

3 (6, 6)

4 (2, 5), (3, 4), (4, 3), (5, 2)

AS ■ 51

Coordinates game.

AS ■ 52

1 acute: A, D;
right: B, F;
obtuse: C, E, G

2 acute: A, D, E, F, G;
right: B;
obtuse: C, H
Child's own work.

AS ■ 53

1 b The frequencies should all be around 8, and should total 50. Player 1 needs four 6s to win. Player 2 needs ten 1s, 2s or 3s to win. So Player 2 has a slightly better chance of winning.

AS ■ 54

1

$\frac{1}{8}$ $\frac{2}{8}$ $\frac{1}{3}$ $\frac{1}{2}$ $\frac{5}{8}$ $\frac{3}{4}$

0 — 1

2

	Today	In my lifetime
Certain		
Likely	I will eat some fruit	
Unlikely		Elephants will become extinct People will have holidays on the moon
Impossible	Both players win at a game of snakes and ladders I will run 1 kilometre in 1 minute	Both players win at a game of snakes and ladders I will run 1 kilometre in 1 minute

AS ■ 55

1 b no chance: I will roll an 8; the dice will not land.
poor chance: I will roll a 6.
even chance: I will roll an odd number.
certain: I will roll a number less than 7.

2 Child's own work.

AS ■ 56

1

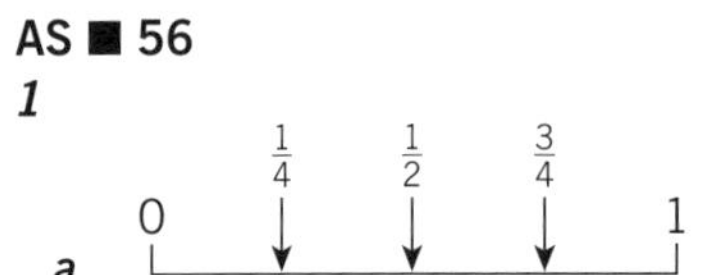

a

$\frac{1}{4}$ $\frac{1}{2}$ $\frac{3}{4}$

0 — 1

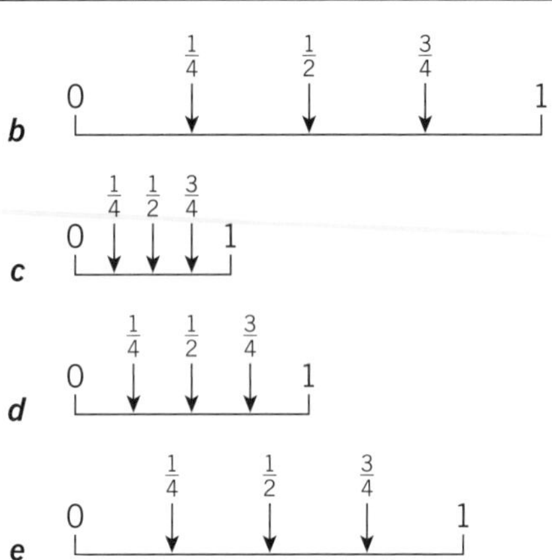

b

$\frac{1}{4}$ $\frac{1}{2}$ $\frac{3}{4}$

0 — 1

c

$\frac{1}{4}$ $\frac{1}{2}$ $\frac{3}{4}$

0 — 1

d

$\frac{1}{4}$ $\frac{1}{2}$ $\frac{3}{4}$

0 — 1

e

$\frac{1}{4}$ $\frac{1}{2}$ $\frac{3}{4}$

0 — 1

Let's play: Possible answers include:
Fair: Each player moves the number of spaces of their dice score.
Unfair: Player 1 moves only for scores of 1, 3 or 5, player 2 only for scores of 2, 4 or 6.

(?) If player 1 uses a 1–6 dice and player 2 a 1–9 dice, player 1 has a poor chance of winning. If players must throw a 9 to reach Home, player 2 always wins.

AS ■ 57
Child's own work.

AS ■ 58
Child's own work.

AS ■ 59
Child's own work.

AS ■ 60
1 Possible answers include:
odd numbers: 1, 3, 5, 7, 9, 11
square numbers: 1, 4, 9, 16, 25, 36
less than 6: 0, 1, 2, 3, 4, 5
between 1000 and 1050: 1001, 1002, 1003, 1047, 1048, 1049

2 a square and odd: 1, 9, 25, 49
square and not odd: 4, 16, 36
not square and odd: 3, 5, 7, 11, 13, 15, 17, 19, 21, 23, 27, 29, 31, 33, 35, 37, 39, 41, 43, 45, 47
not square and not odd: 2, 6, 8, 10, 12, 14, 18, 20, 22, 24, 26, 28, 30, 32, 34, 38, 40, 42, 44, 46, 48

(?) There are fewer square numbers: 64, 81 and 100.